NURSES

for kids

First paperback edition February 2024

Book design by Betty Nguyen & Brandon Pham

ISBN 978-1-957557-24-3 (paperback)

Printed in the United States of America

Published by Black Phoenix Press

www.mdforkids.org

To the friends and family who have supported and loved us unconditionally, and to the mentors who have guided and taught us more than we could have imagined:

Thank you.

Betty & Brandon

NURSE

(NURS)

essential healthcare professional who has completed the necessary education, training, and licensure to provide and coordinate medical care for patients

Nurses are healthcare professionals who provide and coordinate medical care for patients.

Because of their important roles, nurses form the backbone of our healthcare system!

Nurses work on a team alongside doctors, pharmacists, therapists, social workers, and other healthcare professionals.

Nurses work in many different places, like hospitals, clinics, nursing homes, schools, and even people's houses.

Take patient histories

Check vital signs

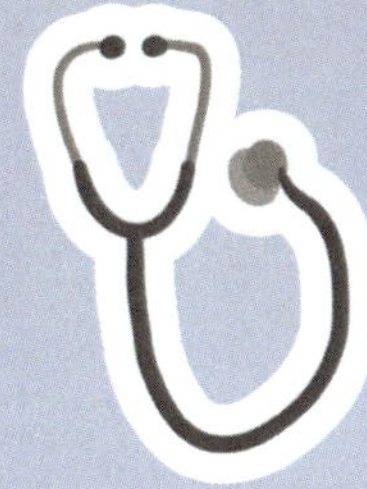

Perform physical exams

Draw lab samples

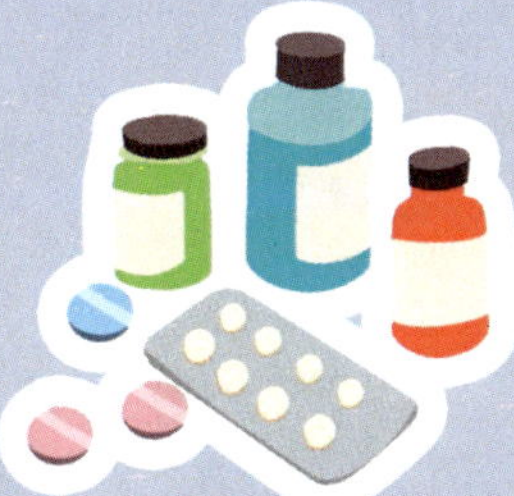

Administer medications

Educate patients

Most nurses are **registered nurses**. They provide direct medical care to patients and have many important responsibilities.

Registered nurses talk to patients to learn more about their health habits, medical problems, and symptoms.

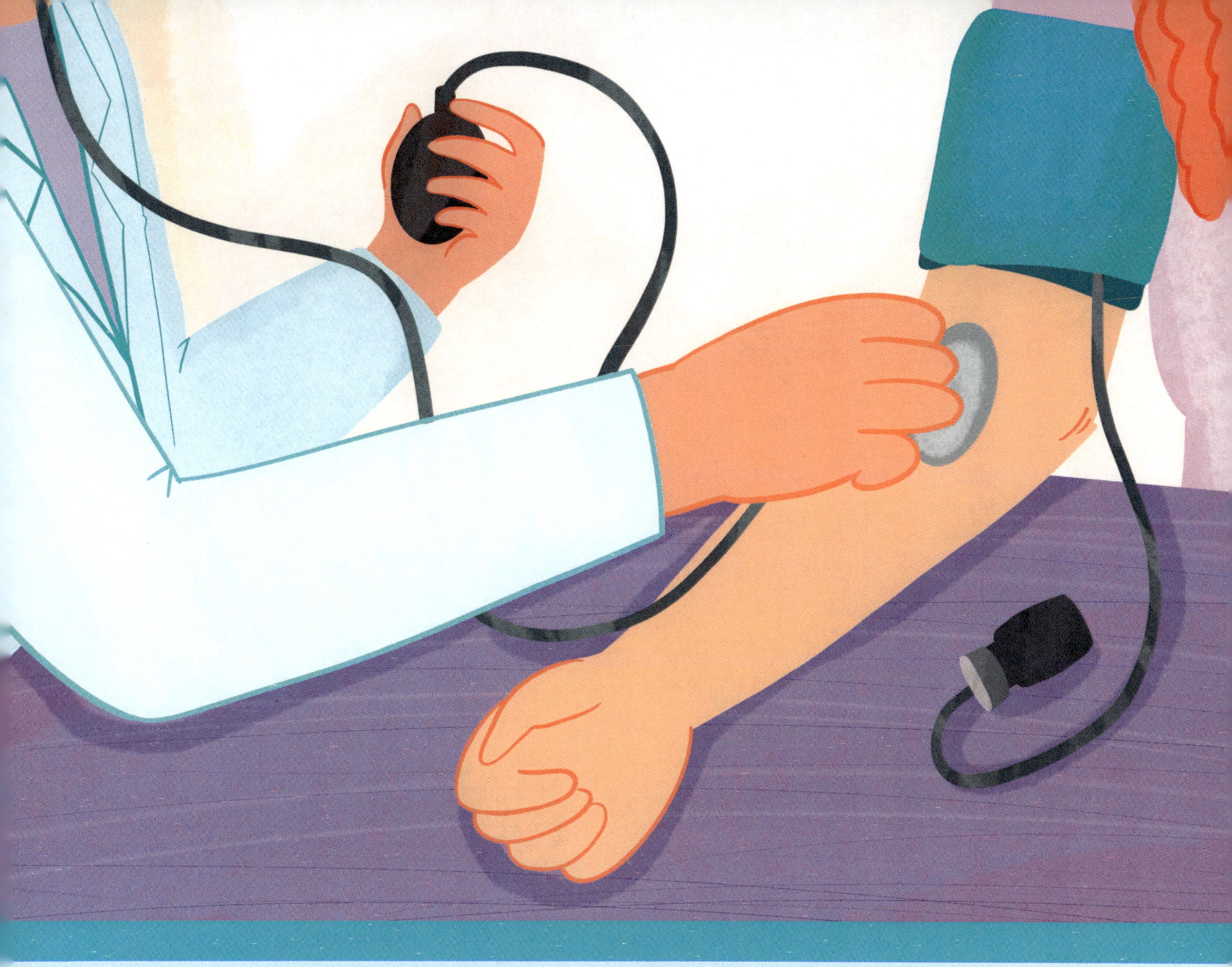

Registered nurses check **vital signs**, such as heart rate and blood pressure, which measure the body's most important functions.

Registered nurses perform **physical exams** on patients, such as listening to their heart and lungs with a stethoscope.

Registered nurses draw blood and urine samples from patients, which provide valuable information about patients' health.

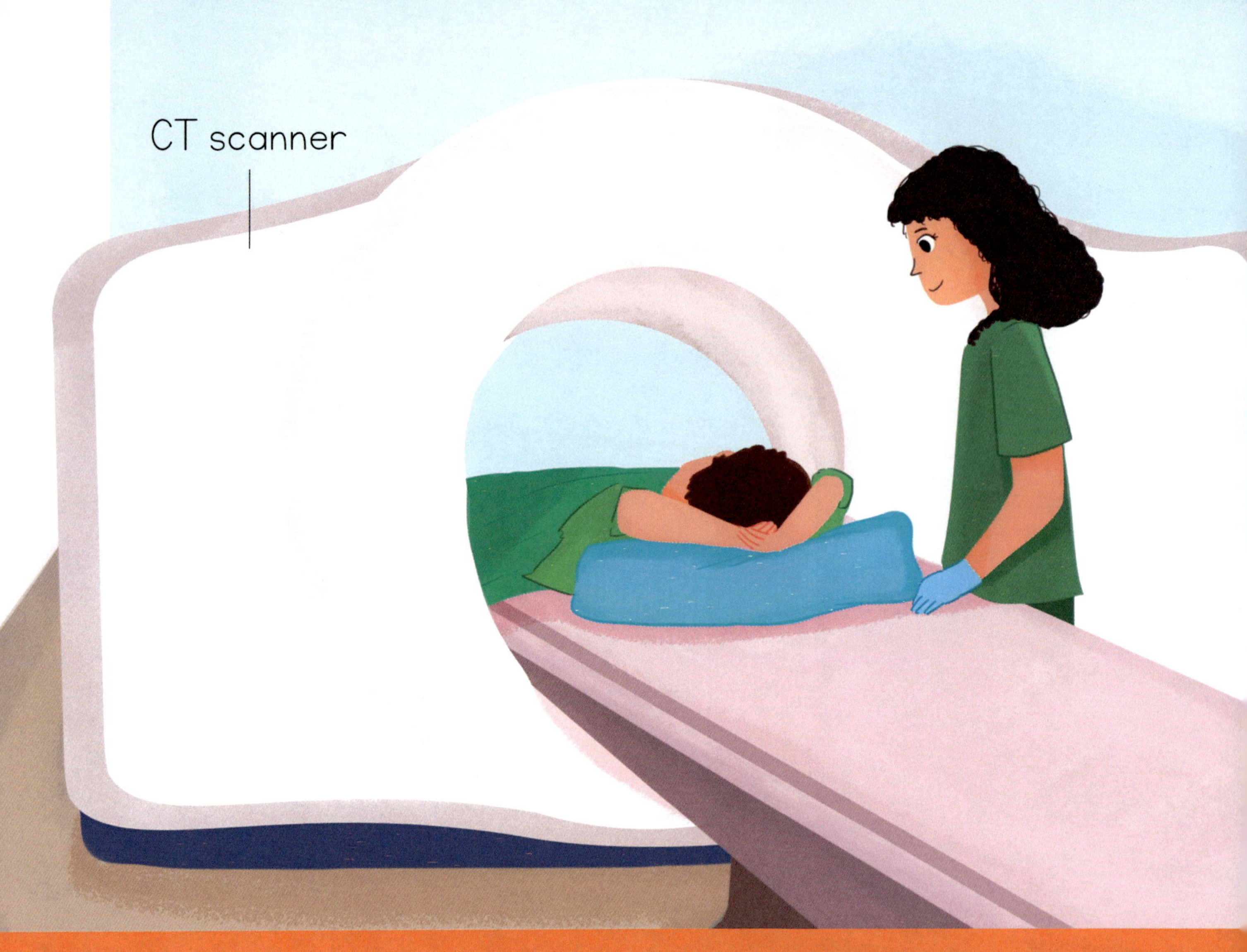

Registered nurses prepare patients for **imaging tests**, such as CT scans, which create pictures of the insides of patients' bodies.

Registered nurses administer medications to help patients recover from illnesses and feel better.

Finally, registered nurses educate patients and family members about their diagnoses and treatment plans.

Some registered nurses complete additional education and training to become **advanced practice registered nurses.**

Nurse practitioner

Doctor

Nurse practitioners are advanced practice registered nurses who share some of the same responsibilities as doctors.

Nurse practitioners diagnose illnesses, which means they can find out what's wrong inside patients' bodies that is making them sick.

They do this by asking questions, performing physical exams, and interpreting diagnostic tests, such as imaging tests and blood samples.

To help patients get better, nurse practitioners prescribe medications and recommend treatment plans.

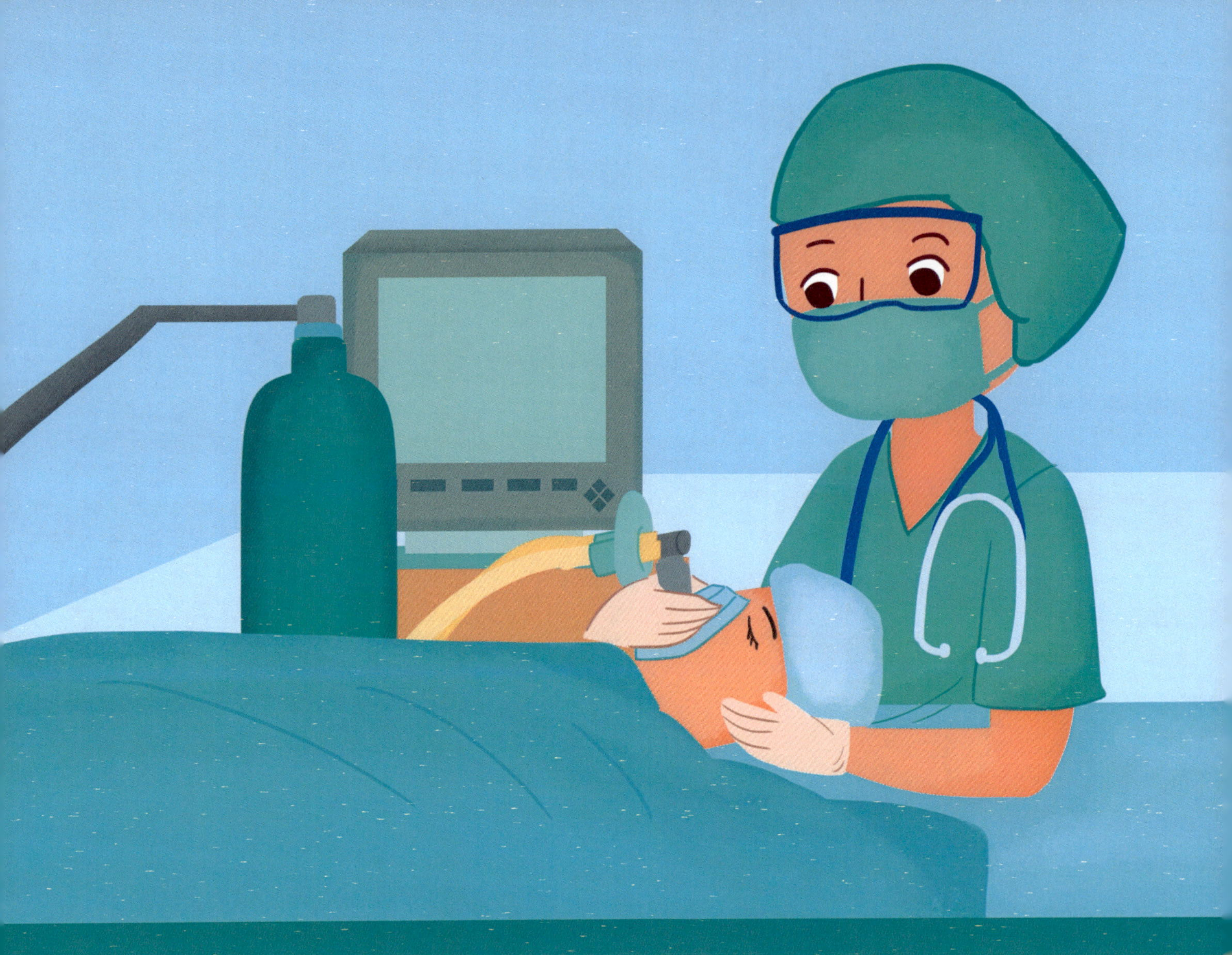

Certified registered nurse anesthetists are advanced practice registered nurses who specialize in providing **anesthesia** to patients.

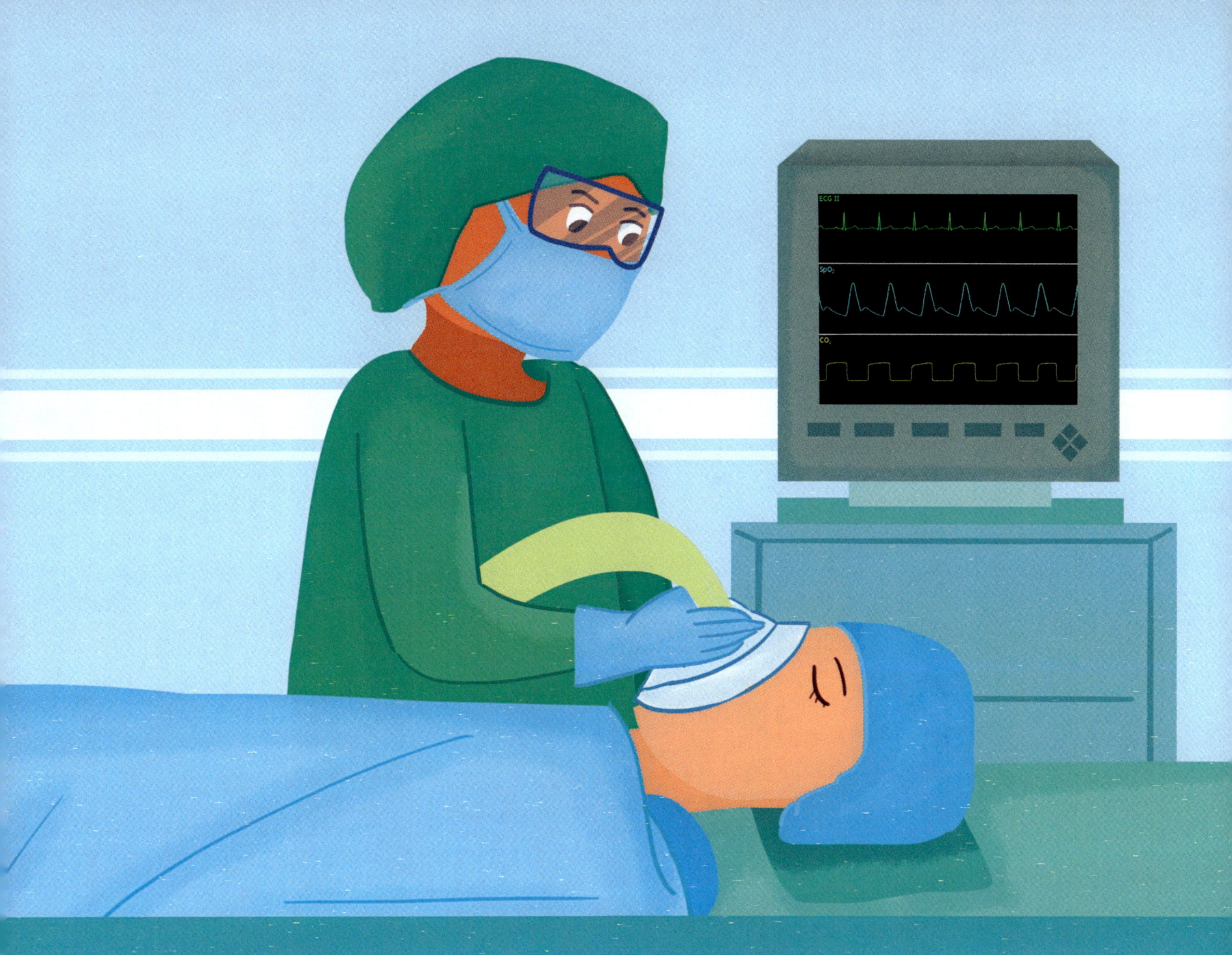

Anesthesia is a special type of medication that makes patients fall asleep and prevents them from feeling pain during **surgery**.

Surgery is a way doctors fix things inside patients' bodies in an **operating room**, which is a sterile environment designed to prevent infection.

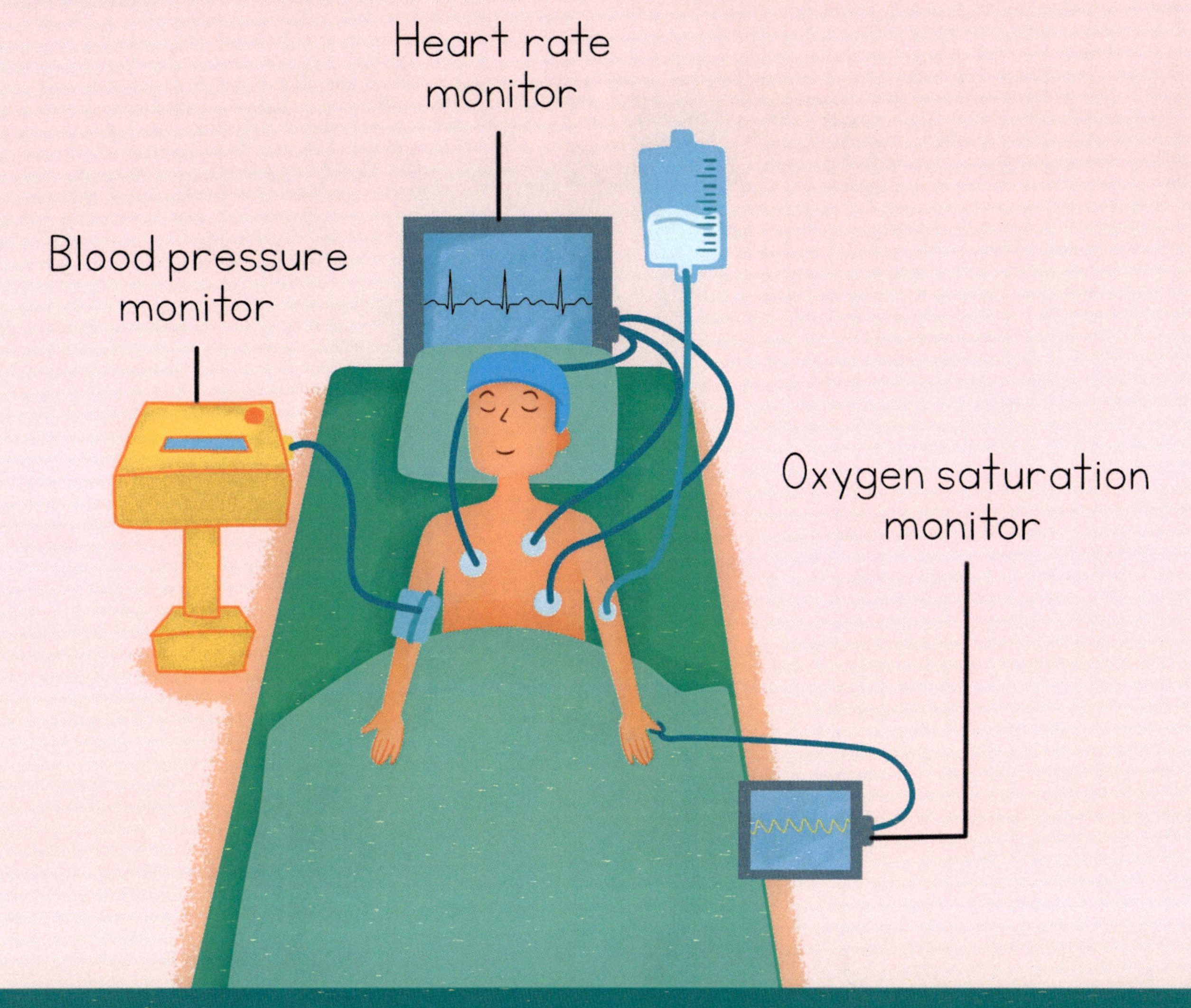

During surgery, certified registered nurse anesthetists make sure that patients remain healthy and stable by monitoring their vital signs.

After surgery, certified registered nurse anesthetists make sure that patients' pain is well controlled by providing medications.

Advanced practice registered nurses are important because they deliver high-quality, accessible, and cost-effective care to patients.

No matter the type, all nurses share a common foundation of kindness, compassion, and dedication to providing the best possible care to patients.

Without nurses, our hospitals, clinics, nursing homes, and operating rooms around the world simply wouldn't be able to function.

YOU'RE A FUTURE NURSE!

Glossary

Advanced practice registered nurse (APRN): highly trained nurse with advanced education and clinical experience, often specializing in roles such as nurse practitioner (NP) or certified registered nurse anesthetist (CRNA)

Certified registered nurse anesthetist (CRNA): type of advanced practice registered nurse with specialized education and training to administer **anesthesia** to patients during surgeries and medical procedures

Imaging test: medical test that uses various technologies, such as X-rays, MRI scans, and CT scans, to create pictures of the insides of patients' bodies

Nurse practitioner (NP): type of advanced practice registered nurse with specialized education and training to provide a wide range of medical services, including the diagnosis and treatment of medical conditions

Operating room: specialized location in a hospital equipped with advanced medical equipment and sterile instruments for performing **surgery**

Physical exam: comprehensive assessment performed by a healthcare professional to evaluate a patient's overall health that involves inspecting, palpating, and listening to different parts of the body

Registered nurse (RN): healthcare professional who has completed the necessary education, training, and licensure to provide and coordinate medical care for patients

Vital signs: clinical measurements of the body's most important functions, such as body temperature, heart rate, breathing rate, blood pressure, and oxygen saturation

Let's review what you learned!

1. What type of medical professional forms the backbone of the healthcare system?
2. What are some examples of other healthcare professionals who work alongside nurses?
3. What are some examples of places where nurses work?
4. What is the most common type of nurse called?
5. What are some of the responsibilities of a registered nurse?
6. Some registered nurses complete additional training and education that grants them greater responsibilities in patient care. What is this type of nurse called?
7. What type of advanced practice registered nurse can diagnose illnesses and prescribe medications, sharing similar responsibilities as doctors?
8. What type of advanced practice registered nurse specializes in providing anesthesia to patients in the operating room?
9. What are three key characteristics of the medical care that advanced practice registered nurses provide to patients?
10. Why does the world need nurses?

Your Answers

1. ____
2. ____
3. ____
4. ____
5. ____
   ____
6. ____
7. ____
8. ____
9. ____
10. ____
    ____

Answer Key

1. Nurses
2. Doctors, pharmacists, therapists, and social workers
3. Hospitals, clinics, nursing homes, schools, and people's houses
4. Registered nurse (RN)
5. Take patient histories, check vital signs, perform physical exams, draw lab samples, prepare patients for imaging tests, administer medications, and educate patients and their family members
6. Advanced practice registered nurse (APRN)
7. Nurse practitioner (NP)
8. Certified registered nurse anesthetist (CRNA)
9. High-quality, accessible, and cost-effective
10. Nurses form the backbone of the healthcare system and play an indispensable role in providing crucial medical care for patients

About the Authors

Betty Nguyen, MD

Betty is a physician specializing in dermatology. She was born in California but spent much of her childhood in Georgia, where she grew up on a chicken farm. Betty studied Biology at UCLA, where she was a Gates Millennium Scholar, and earned her MD from UC Riverside on a full-tuition scholarship. Outside of work, Betty is a certified yoga instructor and licensed scuba diver. She also enjoys journalistic writing and cycling.

Brandon Pham, MD

Brandon is a physician specializing in ophthalmology. He was born and raised in California. Brandon studied Microbiology, Immunology, and Molecular Genetics at UCLA, where he was a Barry Goldwater Scholar, and earned his MD from Stanford. He is passionate about medical education for students of all ages. In his free time, Brandon enjoys traveling, playing tennis, and performing card magic tricks.

Check out the rest of the books in our series!

Website: mdforkids.org

Instagram: @md.for.kids

Made in the USA
Las Vegas, NV
07 October 2024